Remember the Secret

Remember
the
Secret

Elisabeth Kübler-Ross
Illustrations by Heather Preston

Celestial Arts
Berkeley, California

CELESTIAL ARTS
P.O. Box 7327
Berkeley, California 94707

Originally published in hardcover in 1982 by
Celestial Arts (original ISBN 0-89087-332-1).

First Paperback-Printing, 1987

Library of Congress Cataloging in Publication Data

Kübler-Ross, Elisabeth.
Remember the Secret.
Summary: Because she has already discovered
the wonders of God, Suzy understands the true
meaning of her friend's death.
[1. Death—Fiction.   2. Heaven—Fiction]
I. Preston, Heather, ill.   II. Title.
PZ7. 89485Re   [E]   81–68454
ISBN 0-89087-524-3 (pbk.)   AACR2

Manufactured in Singapore

3   4   5 — 91   90

Remember the Secret

Peter and Suzy were good friends. They lived next door to each other and shared many secrets long before they went to school.

They played together in the sandbox beside the honeysuckle vines in Suzy's backyard, and they built beautiful sand castles. No one knew they were not alone. No one heard them talk with two very special friends who told them of many things the grownups did not seem to know about or understand, or maybe had forgotten.

Ever since Suzy's father had died the year before, her mother earned a living by sewing for other people and had a hard time paying the bills. She was often sad and worried. Sometimes she called Suzy into the house even before the sun went down, while Suzy and Peter were in the midst of a visit with their special friends, Theresa and Willy.

Willy always encouraged Suzy to listen to her mother. He also sang to her and made her laugh, telling her that laughter was a wonderful way to make people and God happy. Without Willy to help her, she too would probably have had a sad face like her mother's.

Peter's parents both worked, and Suzy's mother cared for him until his big brother and sister came home from school.

Peter would rush to greet them when the school bus stopped at their gate. He would try to tell them about Theresa, his special friend who looked after him whenever he was alone or with Suzy.

But his brother and sister would just laugh at him.

"He is a little crazy," John would say.

"Wait until he goes to school—he'll stop all these silly stories," Emma would add, hurrying him off to set the table before their parents got home from work.

One night Peter went to bed feeling very sad. *Why don't John and Emma know about Theresa and Willy?* he wondered as he drifted off to sleep.

Suddenly there was a funny sound in his ears, and he rose up toward the ceiling of his bedroom, hovered there a moment, then went right though the roof of his house and over the small town where he lived, up toward the clouds and the stars.

He was flying! He looked back at his house and saw himself sleeping peacefully in his own bed. *How can this be?* Peter wondered. *How can I be home in bed and up here flying at the same time?* But it was wonderful!

He never had felt so happy, so light, so totally free and unafraid. He could not understand any of this, but soon discovered that he could be anywhere he wished with the speed of his thought.

Then he realized that Theresa and Willy were flying alongside him. They smiled with delight to see the big grin lighting his face as he enjoyed the excitement of his first trip out of his body.

Peter thought of Suzy and wanted to share this adventure with her. The colors here were bright and beautiful, and there was a strange, lovely music in the air.

Just thinking of Suzy brought Peter right into her room. He found her sobbing into her pillow. Her mother had scolded her for ''not telling the truth.'' Suzy had only wanted to share with her mother Willy's visits to the sandbox, and what he told her about making people and God happy with laughter!

Suddenly Willy was right next to Suzy and gently stretched out his hand and, before she knew it, Suzy followed Peter and Theresa into the other world.

Willy led them, and as they floated he sang:

''Come to my world, my loves.

Come to the land where there is peace;

Come to the land where there is love;

Come to the land without pain, without tears.

Come to my world, my loves.''

Suzy and Peter had never heard a more beautiful voice. They had never seen such wondrous colors. And they moved along quite easily as if they had been able to fly all their lives.

When they stopped, they were in a place with flowers everywhere, smelling sweeter than honeysuckle. There were many people there, of all ages, sizes and colors. They all looked beautiful and were very happy together—there was no pushing, throwing things, blaming, scolding or fighting. Things were as they could and should be, Peter thought, but he didn't really understand why it was never this peaceful and loving in his own home.

Theresa and Willy led them to a patch of grass at the edge of a waterfall. The waterfall seemed to create special mirror images for them in a pool.

Theresa and Willy tossed their clothes onto the grass and splashed into the crystal-clear pool. They invited Suzy and Peter to join them.

This was even nicer than their visits in the sandbox! In this place no one thought it strange that they wore no clothes. Peter wondered for a moment if his father would be angry if he saw them now.

Willy knew every thought Peter had, and he told both Peter and Suzy in a gentle voice that God had created our bodies and that we should be proud of them; we should never compare them as less or more beautiful—the beauty is in their uniqueness, and there are no two alike in the whole galaxy!

Suzy wanted to know what a galaxy was, and for a long time they talked, listened, laughed and shared together.

When they were together, they did not make sounds with their lips and tongues, but everyone could understand and respond to the thoughts of the other. It reminded Peter of two children he had seen once on the bus who could neither speak nor hear and had communicated with each other silently, except that here in this world you didn't even have to move your fingers.

Theresa slowly stepped out of the water and pointed her arm to a faraway light.

"Let's show them some of the stars of our galaxy!"

And off they went, dancing on a thousand stars.

It was neither cold nor warm, neither dark nor very bright. While they danced and laughed and traveled with the speed of their thoughts, Theresa and Willy continued their teachings:

"God created this world millions of years ago, and there were many animals, all with different shapes and qualities. God gave them all a chance to grow, to alter, to adapt and adjust to changes in their world.

"Humans alone seemed to make it through hot and cold weather, through dry spells or snow and ice. They learned to share, to build shelters, to put skins and leaves on their bodies, and to grow faster than any other animal in the understanding of the world in which they lived.

"And so it came to pass that God called them back to Him and revealed a great gift for all people.

"Henceforth He would create new souls and put them into this galaxy. They would all be a little part of Him; and they would be given yet another gift—the gift of free choice!

"They would look over the planet Earth to find the spot they liked most. They would decide what they wanted to learn, what they wanted to become. They would consider carefully how they could make this world a better place, how they could contribute to the well-being of everyone. All the good they did would become the gifts they would bring back to God when they had completed their tasks—their self-chosen destinies—and returned home to their Creator, back to God where all of us began.

"What you are is a gift of God. Treasure it. You are special and beautiful, all of you, each one a different facet of the Divinity. . ."

"What you make of your life is the gift that you bring back to God, to the Source, the Creator of all life," Theresa added softly.

Her eyes sparkled and her face beamed. Her white gown had wide sleeves and, as she stretched out her arms, the borders on her collar and her sleeves glittered as if covered with pure gold.

It was time for Peter and Suzy to return to bed, she said, and Willy sang a last favorite song for them.

"Remember now, when you wake up you will feel very rested and happy. You will think of it as a dream, but you must always remember that we are beside you, even if you cannot see us. Let that be your special secret.

"Remember the love and peace of this—our world—and remember never to criticize or to judge other people. They are all learning and growing. Try always to understand and love each person you meet."

They hugged each other, and Peter and Suzy had never experienced such love and warmth. When they awakened, they were back in their own bedrooms.

The summer came and passed, the leaves started to fall, and Suzy and Peter saw less of each other. Suzy would start school soon. But Peter had become pale and weak, and his family doctor thought it best to have some tests done in a big hospital in the next city.

Suzy missed him and would have liked to send a note to him in the hospital, but she could not yet write. She could not ask her mother to write for her, as she would have had to leave out the most important part—that she had a message from Theresa and Willy telling her that Peter would join them soon.

Suzy was sitting alone in the sandbox, trying very hard to think of a way to send a message to Peter. She thought of all she had learned from her special friends, and it suddenly occurred to her that she could visit Peter in the hospital during her sleep.

If she were able to fly from star to star, from the waterfall to the garden of the beautiful, happy people, then she should also be able to fly to the hospital.

Suzy knew that children were not allowed to visit patients in the hospital. *A stupid rule*, she said to herself, and then she remembered what Theresa had said about not being critical and judgmental. She would never need to be critical of others and their rules if she could learn unconditional love.

Suzy's mother tucked her little daughter into bed that night, and kissed her gently. She wondered at how Suzy had changed in the past few months, how full of smiles and laughter and happiness she had been lately, and how eagerly she was going to bed that night. For the first time in a long while, Suzy's mother smiled.

Although she still missed her husband, it seemed less lonesome to her now. *If only Suzy would stop thinking about those imaginary playmates of hers!* But soon she would be going to school and would probably forget all about Theresa and Willy, she thought as she left the room.

As Suzy drifted off to sleep, she felt a gentle touch on her shoulder and heard a soft voice saying, ''Peter knows; he will soon be with us. . .''

Suzy tossed and turned in her bed. She wondered if Peter's parents knew where he would soon be going. She also wondered why grownups did not know that we all go to the beautiful place when God calls us, where no one ever gets punished for being bad, where no one knows any pain or grief or sorrow, and where everyone can dance from star to star. . .

On Sunday, Peter came home from the hospital, and Suzy's mother took her next door to visit with him for a very few minutes. He looked strange and different. His lips were parched, and he had big shadows under his eyes. Suzy slipped a few grains of sand and a bit of honeysuckle into his hand. Maybe Peter would know what she was trying to tell him.

Peter's eyes stared at her, and it seemed that he had trouble talking or thinking. Suzy knew that he would die soon.

The sand slipped through his fingers, and the honeysuckle rested on his bedsheet. Suddenly a faint smile came over his face, and he whispered, ''Remember the secret?''

She nodded and gently touched his warm hand, which still tried to clutch onto the last bits of sand. Her eyes were full of tears and, before she had a chance to say goodbye, she was gently pulled away from his bed and led out into the hallway.

Remember the secret echoed in her ears.

A week later, Suzy's mother took her to Peter's funeral. She stood in line between many grownups and saw only his face for a few moments when she walked by the casket.

His hands were folded over his white shirt, his eyes were closed, and his lips were very pale. But Suzy knew that this was not the real Peter! He had left his body as a butterfly leaves the cocoon when it is time to graduate, time to fly!

Suzy closed her eyes. She heard the grownups cry and whisper, but she was somewhere else with her thoughts. She knew that Peter was with Theresa and Willy, and she heard Willy's beautiful voice singing:

> "Come to my world, my loves.
> Come to the land where there is peace;
> Come to the land where there is love;
> Come to the land without pain, without tears.
> Come to my world, my loves."

She saw Theresa's white robe and her long brown hair and her outstretched hand. She saw Peter between them—beaming, laughing, singing with Willy. Somehow she knew that Peter would visit her with Theresa and Willy from time to time. He would help her through lonely times when her mother was tired or when her schoolwork seemed hard, or when she was alone in the sandbox by the flowers, with her eyes closed, recalling his whispered, "Remember the secret. . ."

Suzy was only vaguely aware of the church service. Almost all the grownups cried, but she just could not cry. She was remembering the wonderful times they had shared together. They had never been mean to each other, they had never pushed or kicked each other. She and Peter had always remembered the love they felt when they were with Theresa and Willy, and they had always hoped to become as beautiful as their guardian angels, for now Suzy was sure that was who Theresa and Willy were.

Just as she pondered that, Suzy heard the pastor say, ". . . .and Peter is now an angel. . ." And she knew it was all right to think of Peter that way, too.

She stole a look at her mother and saw tears in her eyes. Another thought came to her: perhaps she could talk with her mother about Theresa and Willy after all, if she explained that they were angels—guardian angels. And perhaps she could tell her that somewhere in Theresa and Willy's world her father was an angel too, happy in a world of love and peace.

And then a bright flutter of pictures crossed Suzy's mind. She seemed to see herself in school, growing up, growing old even—and all through those years she would have three faithful friends visiting her—Theresa, Willy, and Peter, her guardian angels. And she knew now that her father would come to her too, whenever she needed him.

Again she heard Peter's familiar whisper. And this time she answered him, "Of course. Of course I'll remember," she called silently.

"I'll always remember the secret."

Elisabeth Kübler-Ross

Photograph: Ken Ross